D1500258

COLLECTORS' PIECES

ALL KINDS OF SMALL BOXES

John Bedford

WALKER AND COMPANY

NEW YORK

Library of Congress Catalog Card Number: 65–22127

First published in the United States of America in
1965 by Walker and Company, a division of
Publications Development Corporation

Reprinted 1966
Third Printing 1968

Printed in Hong Kong

Contents

Introduction

If in some very special heaven there is a register of the things which people have given each other, small boxes must rank high on the list. Men of all ranks and stations have given them to each other and also to women; and women, sometimes rashly, have given them to men. Kings have used them to convey gratitude to courtiers and honour to ambassadors; States and cities, grateful for rescue from sacking or oblivion, have bestowed them upon generals and admirals. Heroic deeds have been commemorated with them, secrets confided to their hidden panels. Most of them have changed hands many times, and the tiniest of them will at some time or other have perhaps carried an intolerably heavy cargo of joys or sighs.

One can also find in these small, exquisite things the pleasure and pride of the craftsman in his work; and if one is impressed by the spectacular pieces in gold, silver and precious stone, one should remember that those which have borne little cost beyond the labour of carving and making are often hardly less exciting.

This little book tries to give a taste of the delight which can be found in the study of small boxes, and offers some preliminary guidance to those who would like to start collecting them.

The pleasures of doing so will be obvious; as to the cost, there is a proverb known to the Chinese—themselves great makers and collectors of boxes—'If you have two loaves of bread, sell one and buy a narcissus.'

1. Uses for Small Boxes

Before we talk of the nature of boxes themselves, of the kinds of materials they were made of, and the people who made them, let us first consider their purposes.

It will not take us long to discover that in any age the most insatiable consumer of boxes has been the toilet table. Queen Jezebel painted her face very carefully; Cleopatra would have faced an array of artful aids when she prepared herself to meet the conquering Caesars. Queen Elizabeth I showed ambassadors a youthful face for many years with her paint and powder and wigs. In *Love's Labour's Lost* Shakespeare notes:

> *Your mistresses dare never come in rain*
> *For fear their colours should be washed away.*

Ladies of those days had to suffer to be beautiful even more than they do today, for some of these pre-Rubinstein cosmetics were tricky things. The usual ingredient for lip salve and rouge was a kind of white lead, mixed with colour and common whiting; this could give you pains in the stomach and head, dizziness and even blindness. The Gunning sisters, celebrated beauties of the eighteenth century, whose portraits appear on enamel boxes, are said to have lost their looks, and at least one of them her life, through using white lead. The wonder is that the boxes themselves have survived.

Many boxes and pots were needed, for these powders and unguents were often home-mixed, sometimes from the most surprising things. If you want to know how Elizabeth I continued to astonish the ambassadors with her youthfulness, here is what she used for a cleansing lotion: two new-laid eggs *and* their shells, burnt alum, powdered sugar,

5

borax and poppy seeds, all beaten very finely with a pint of water 'that runs from under the wheel of the mill'.

In England in the early seventeenth century make-up on the whole was restrained; and life became even more austere during the Commonwealth. But with the Restoration, and the Merry Monarch on the throne, bringing with him French manners and tastes, discretion took a back seat. Dressing tables became loaded with handsome accessories to beauty in gold and silver, Chinese porcelain and Spanish leather, perfumed wood from Oporto, glass from Venice and the Levant. When important young ladies married, they expected to be given huge 'toilet sets' of twenty or thirty pieces.

PATCH BOXES
Along with the powder and ointment boxes stood the *boîte*

Marie-Antoinette's casket in rock crystal and silver filigree. Her crowned monogram is engraved on the underside, and the base is formed of lapis lazuli and agate plaques set in silver-gilt foliage cagework. Said to have been a wedding present, it was sold at Sotheby's for £500 in 1961. (Sotheby & Co.)

6

à mouche for patches. These were small black pieces of taffeta or thin red Spanish leather, worn to provide the damask cheek with the 'love spot' of Venus. They did seem to lend a sparkle to the eye, as one discovers even today at fancy dress balls; they also helped to hide a blemish or an incipient spot.

Patch-wearing is often thought of as being unique to the eighteenth century, but in fact it began in the sixteenth, and became extraordinarily widespread in the seventeenth. Patches were not only circular but came in all kinds of shapes—crescent, diamonds, squares; some ladies would even have a miniature coach and six driving across their foreheads. In Queen Anne's reign they were sometimes worn as party favours, Whig ladies patching on the right side of the face and Tory supporters on the left: presumably non-political ladies patched on both sides at once or not at all. Patches were enormously in favour when Pope was writing his 'Rape of the Lock' in 1712, for in showing Belinda at the sacred rite of her toilet, with 'each silver vase in mystic order laid', he speaks also of her 'Puffs, powders, patches, Bibles, *billets-doux*'.

How are we to distinguish the boxes so used? A powder box, presumably, will usually be found with room for a puff or some other instrument of application. A patch box needs to be shallow, and at the same time large enough for two fingers to grope for the slender pieces of taffeta or leather. Sometimes they have loose lids; but one would also need patch boxes with hinged ones, for repairs when the heat of candles had undone a patch or for use on coach journeys around the countryside—it would never have done for highwaymen not to have seen one at one's best. The *boîte à rouge* explains itself, and sometimes this was combined in a box with interior hinged lids having compartments for rouge for the cheek and kohl for the eyes, a mirror and a tiny brush—the vanity box of those days. But these boxes come in great variety of shape and size, as we shall see when we come to discuss materials and makers.

Some articles in the boudoir leave no doubt of their purpose. Little caskets, often in the form of the miniature commodes of the period, would obviously have held trinkets and jewellery. Workboxes are perhaps too large to concern us here, but there are the small needle-cases which go with them, sometimes in the form of a little book with two leaves of red cloth and gilt metal mounts. There may be a bodkin case, perhaps cylindrical, embellished with enamelled printing of romantic ruins.

There were, too, little boxes carried about the person, for example, the *étui*. This might be suspended by a ring from the châtelaine, which some ladies were still old-fashioned enough to wear around the waist. In it would be all manner of items needed for the comfort and convenience of the wearer—the same things, very largely, which these days so inexplicably astonish gentlemen by their multitude when they come cascading out of upset handbags. There were—though not all in the same *étui*—paper knives, pencil holders, tweezers, scissors, memorandum tablets of ivory, small brass spoons, penknives (which really were *pen*knives then, being designed to sharpen and trim quill pens), cut-glass scent bottles, lacing-pins, corkscrews (for perfume bottles only, one hopes), compasses, tooth-picks, bodkins, six-inch folding rules (for dressmaking), and two-pronged forks, sometimes with a detachable handle into which all the other items in the *étui* will fit. An *étui* may also be combined with another item such as a spy-glass.

We shall speak of vinaigrettes more appropriately in their place, but there were also comfit boxes or *bonbonnières*, sometimes called *drageoirs*, to hold little sweets or cachous to sweeten the breath. Again, when out visiting it was nice to carry with you a little silver or enamel box containing a nutmeg and grater, so that when you were offered hot toddy, mulled wine or October ale, or perhaps custards and other sweets, you could flavour the offering to your own taste.

The habit of sniffing up finely powdered tobacco seems to have started in France soon after Jean Nicot introduced the weed there from America: it is his name as well as the island of Tobago which has become associated with it. It was used here in court circles in Shakespeare's day; the tempestuous Hotspur, in *Henry IV*, describes how, when he was busy slaughtering Scots at Holmeden,

> *Came there a certain lord, neat, and trimly dressed,*
> *Fresh as a bridegroom; and his chin new reap'd*
> *Show'd like a stubble-land at harvest-home:*
> *He was perfumed like a milliner;*
> *And 'twixt his finger and his thumb he held*
> *A pouncet-box, which ever and anon*
> *He gave his nose and took't way again;*
> *Who therewith angry, when it next came there,*
> *Took it in snuff. . . .*

But the habit does not seem to have become widely practised for another fifty years, when tobacco addicts not only snuffed but, apparently, 'chawed'. Pepys confides to his diary on one occasion: 'It put me into such an ill conception of myself that I was forced to buy some roll-tobacco to smell and chaw, which took away my apprehension.'

This gives us a clue to the very earliest sort of snuffboxes, which were, in fact, small portable snuff factories. Fifty years before Pepys wrote his diary entry, Scots accompanying James I to London at the time of their first conquest of England had brought with them something they called a 'sneeshing miln'. Now known as a Scottish mull, this was a contrivance made with native frugality from a ram's horn, its inside being cut with sharp ridges from top to bottom, so providing a grater on which one could scrape a plug of tobacco. The horn had a cap of silver or ivory, sometimes mounted with a cairngorm, and perhaps engraved with the owner's initials. One still finds them in junk shops fitted with

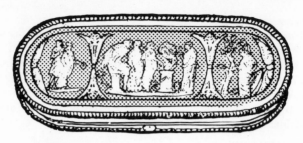

Wedgwood jasper ware cameo on an ivory patch box inlaid with cut-steel beads. (Josiah Wedgwood & Sons.)

a snuff spoon, a small mallet, a rake and a hare's foot for dusting the snuff from one's moustache and beard—remember that we are in the age of Vandyke!

SNUFF READY-MADE

On reaching the capital the 'sneeshing miln' started to put on airs. It became a box containing at one end a plug of tobacco—a *carotte*, as it was called from its shape—and at the other a rasp or grater, and as time went on this became more and more elaborate and sophisticated. There were richly carved cases of various hardwoods inlaid and otherwise decorated, or perhaps of silver or ivory; there was a

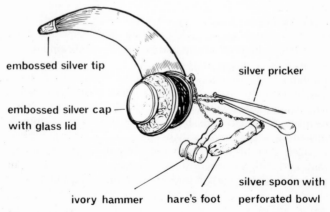

Scottish 'sneeshing miln', ancestor of the snuffbox. (Kenneth D. Foster Esq., M.B.E.)

Châtelaine with manicure nécessaire and two vinaigrette boxes. Firegilt copper from eighteenth-century Germany.

swinging lid and a recess under the grater with a groove through which the snuff was poured on to the back of the hand. Huge rasps of this kind became the conventional sign of the snuff merchant—and this itself signalled the next change in the habits of nosologists, as they were at that time termed.

For as the habit of snuff-taking spread, it became more practicable to buy the snuff ready ground by the merchant with his outsize mill. Some say that this process was hastened in England by the fact that in the early 1700s one of our British admirals captured several ships' cargoes of Spanish and Cuban snuff, which were sold for the prize money at very low prices. At all events, the market was now well provided with hundreds of varieties of ready-ground snuff, from rappee (Fr. *tabac râpé*: rasped) to brands perfumed with oils of bergamot, jasmine, violet, lily of the valley, civet, musk and even wine. The various kinds were obtainable under such exotic names as Bolongaro, Façon de Paris, King's Carotte, Jesuit's Bran and Masulipatam.

For using the pocket snuffbox, of course, there was a whole set of rules and requirements. The *Spectator* in 1711 carried an advertisement for a kind of charm school where, for two hours every day, young merchants around the Royal Exchange in London could learn the ceremony of the snuffbox, being taught the rules for offering snuff to a stranger, a friend or a mistress, 'with an explanation of the careless, the scornful, the politic, and the surly pinch, and the gestures proper to each of them'. But most people simply tapped the box three times, to ensure that the snuff was shaken away from the lid, put a pinch on the back of the left hand or on the thumbnail and then applied the nose, which thereupon 'took it in snuff'.

Who came first, the snuff-taker or the smoker? Tobacco, for the pipe, has called for boxes ever since the days of Nicot and Raleigh. So too, in latter days, have cigarettes: cigar smokers seem to prefer to call their containers cases. But there are collectable small ornamental match boxes, from both before and after the invention of the safety match.

What other kinds of boxes are there? Letters and parchment rolls have used boxes for a long time, so have gloves and knives. Caddies, after all, are boxes—I insist on the term even for porcelain ones. Music can be found upon opening the lids of boxes large and small, as can incense and holy relics. Money is put into them—and taking it out has destroyed thousands of irreplaceable ones. The Japanese have carried medicines in collapsible boxes, and the English lengths of string in circular ones. But perhaps the boxiest box of them all is the one, made by the Chinese with astonishing skill, which serves only to contain smaller and ever smaller boxes.

But now let us look at some history and some materials.

2. 'Vieux Paris'

If cost be any criterion our procession of little boxes will start in Paris in the eighteenth century. There, in and around the courts of the three kings Louis XIV, XV, XVI, spanning the years from the death of the first in 1715 to the execution of the third in 1793, there existed a small society with a taste for beautiful things, rich and powerful enough to indulge itself, and having at its command a race of craftsmen eager to make their fortunes. Boxes were made in France before this era, and also again elsewhere, when the twilight of the Revolution had been swept away by Napoleon; but nothing ever quite rivalled this period for producing boxes and other *objets d'art* in what was almost a fury of luxury and extravagance. 'Vieux Paris', in this sense, means the best.

Many boxes made by the goldsmiths and jewellers, the enamellers and the miniature painters of this period are to be seen in fabulous treasure houses like the Louvre in Paris, the Metropolitan Museum in New York, the Victoria and Albert Museum and the Wallace Collection in London. More will be found in the shops of the specialist antique dealers; others appear in the larger salerooms; and just occasionally a hoard of them is unloaded at some rich man's death. In October 1963, for example, the collection of gold snuffboxes, miniatures and other objects of *vertu* gathered together by the late René Fribourg was sold at Sotheby's for a total of £142,187, or $398,123—an average of over £400 for each lot. The highest individual price was the £14,000 ($39,200) paid for a Louis XV gold and enamel snuffbox made in Paris in 1749 by Jean Moynat; interestingly enough, this box bore no grandiose design or lavish jewelling but a simple, though exquisitely done, pattern in brilliantly coloured enamels of carnations, peonies, roses and cornflowers.

(Above) *Snuffbox in* Zwischengoldglas *with hunting and fishing scenes in gold on a red background. German c. 1700.* (Sotheby & Co.)

(Below) *Dresden gold and hardstone snuffbox by Johann Christian Neuber. The flowers are in various hardstones including agate, jasper and lapis lazuli.*

Gold and enamel were the chief materials used for these exquisite boxes. Of enamel more will be said presently, for it was used universally; but the goldsmiths of eighteenth-century France were never surpassed at their jobs. Their chief art was to produce gold of different colours in combination on the same piece. They called it *quatrecouleur*; but this must not be taken to imply that there were always as many as four colours or indeed as few; up to eight different shades could be achieved. Fine differences of tint or tone are already present in gold, according to its source; and by careful alloying with other metals, these differences could be accentuated. For example, a reddish gold alloyed with copper produced a coppery red; a pale yellow gold alloyed with silver would give a greenish gold; with iron, a bluish shade.

These various golds were carved by *ciseleurs*, some of whom became famous. Until the Revolution gold boxes bore hallmarks, a complete set including the master's mark, the crowned year letter, the '*Ferme-Générale*' mark and the charge and discharge marks. Year marks followed an alphabetical sequence, as do our own, with a change in style for each cycle of years: 'D' indicates the year 1720,

Louis XV gold and mother-of-pearl scent casket set with vignettes of agate, chased gold animals and putti; it holds six glass scent bottles and a funnel; there is a mirror in the lid.

when the '*Ferme-Générale*' system of tax-gathering was set up; the rights to collect taxes were sold as sinecures.

Boxes which were bought and kept simply as *objets d'art* —as a surprising number were, to judge by their 'mint' state—show their marks boldly enough, but those carried in the pocket have often had theirs rubbed away with time and use.

The style of this gold carving is obviously important in setting a date to a piece. Up to about mid-century, or just after, the extravagant, asymmetrical designs of the rococo held sway; with these boxes, the elaborate carving as often as not ignored the break of a lid, and used the thumb-piece as part of the design. But Louis Seize gave his name to a restrained approach to design, inspired by the renewed interest in classical themes: only after the Revolution is

Swiss gold snuffbox in the form of a peach, enamelled brilliantly in pink, yellow and green, with two translucent green enamel leaves. About 1800. (Sotheby & Co.)

there a return to lavish decoration, and then it is with the quite different feeling of 'Empire'.

Louis XIV was as firm an opponent of snuff-taking as James I had been of tobacco-smoking a century before. Courtiers at Versailles were therefore obliged to disguise their *tabatières* as *boîtes de portraits*, that is to say little boxes containing miniature portraits. Later in the century, when the *Grand Monarque* had gone to his long home, these portraits, painted on ivory, would be mounted on the outside of the box. The work of Rosalba Carriera was famous throughout the first half of the century; so too was that of Adolph Hall, a Swiss, and the Blarenberghe family, of Dutch origin.

Apart from boxes in the conventional ovals and oblongs, the round ones with lift-off lids, the cartouche shapes and the very rare triangles, there are the *fantaisies*, in all kinds of shapes and guises. Some represent portable hip baths, or woven baskets of fruit; there are satchels, tricorne hats, sabots, sedan chairs, wine casks and travelling trunks. There are also boxes made from natural curiosities like shells, fossils and petrified wood.

The famous and very rare 'Montgolfier' boxes commemorate the balloon ascent in 1783; Admiral Vernon, of Portobello and pottery fame, appears on another series; while many are the 'Freedom Boxes' awarded to national heroes by grateful towns and cities—the Duke of Wellington was given dozens by admirers, from emperors and kings downwards.

Some of the more precious boxes were used as tokens of payment for services rendered—often of a very special nature—and sold back to the maker at a discount for the cash which it would have been undignified for him to accept; then out it would go again into circulation for further use in this way. A gold box, in fact, became a standard method of transferring value, and huge sums were spent on giving them to ambassadors and statesmen on the occasion of important treaties—they were called *boîtes diplomatiques*.

Dresden was another famous source of boxes, at first of the famous porcelain, the secret of which was newly discovered in the early years of the century. Some of these were gold-mounted; but the goldsmiths of Dresden are chiefly noted for their work with semi-precious stones, often hollowed out of solid pieces of bloodstone, carnelian, chalcedony, sardonyx, rock crystal or the like; many such boxes took the form of animals, with jewels as eyes. They also used the so-called Neuber technique, whereby inlays of polished stones were used to create original and interesting

Fabergé gold and enamel nécessaire *in black and gold strips over a translucent strawberry red ground; it carries compartments for cigarettes, snuff, powder and lipstick. By the workmaster Henrik Wigstrom.* (Sotheby & Co.)

patterns. In the works set up in Berlin by Frederick the Great—who owned 1,700 snuffboxes of his own—hardstones were used, but in a more versatile way, attractive pictures being built up in mosaic.

Vienna, Strasbourg, St Petersburg and Moscow were all famous for their boxes, but perhaps the most individual were those from Switzerland. The goldsmiths and enamellers there concentrated on the markets of the Near and Far East—whither, of course, they had long been sending their extraordinarily fine watches.

The orientals adored boxes with fine painting surrounded by borders and festoons in daringly brilliant colours, and eagerly bought the series of *fantaisie* boxes in the flattened outlines of birds and beasts, flowers, fruits and insects. Butterfly boxes, with the wings hinged centrally, are famous, and these are among the many combination musical and snuff or other boxes made in Switzerland. Perhaps the most delicately spectacular of these are the 'singing-bird' boxes, which have a spring which causes a miniature songster to appear and sing his song through tiny bellows, turning his head and fluttering his wings, all in the most life-like way.

What was in one sense a re-creation of eighteenth-century craftsmanship appears on the celebrated pieces made by Carl Fabergé, the Frenchman of Huguenot origin, who set up at the Imperial Russian Court and organized there a team of craftsmen of unique abilities. His jewelled Easter eggs, presented to the Imperial family every year, are both famous and fabulous—one was sold a few years ago at Sotheby's for £11,000 ($30,800).

Fabergé made exquisite use in his boxes of hardstones, also of nugget or rough-cast gold; his range extends from the most austere modern or neo-classical styles to the most ornate or the grimly humorous—boxes exactly representing a ripe tomato, or a potato, or a gorilla's head come to him quite naturally.

From the era of the elegancies and extravagancies of 'Vieux Paris' comes also the world of porcelain. Born in the age when the grandeur of the baroque was transforming itself into the frivolity of the rococo, it has never really been happy since. Dresden porcelain has already been mentioned, and fittingly comes first, since it was there or at nearby Meissen that the young alchemist Böttger, shut up in a fortress, rediscovered independently the secret of making true porcelain, hitherto known only to the Chinese.

Porcelain boxes with hinged lids have to be set with metal mounts and sometimes they are additionally decorated with jewels, precious stones, gold and silver, and other materials. Often these German boxes are set with a portrait or other plaque in relief.

The great French factory at Sèvres was virtually ruled by the Pompadour—and as she is reputed to have had a snuffbox for every day of the year it may be imagined that the establishment turned out many boxes. The Capo di Monte factory founded at Naples made little ones in the style of the delicious *blanc de chine* porcelain of Te Hua—which itself offers boxes in its various tones of white, from warm pink to a smoky grey.

The 'toys' in Chelsea porcelain are famous, and they include *bonbonnières* in engaging shapes, like those shown on pages 36-7. Many of them have lids of enamelled copper, presumably from Bilston or from across the river at Battersea. These Chelsea boxes may have been copied from Continental models, but their mood is entirely English—even if some of them have quaintly misspelt mottoes in French. Many collectors in the past have found them on their Continental travels, so they were evidently exported a great deal.

3. Enamels

All kinds of materials are called 'enamel' nowadays, from housepaint to fingernail varnish. But in the sense we are now using it is a kind of glass paste, containing metal colouring matter, not at all unlike that used in making paste jewellery. It is applied in one form or another to the surface of an article, whether it be a Chinese box of brass, a 'Battersea' box of copper, or a Worcester teapot of porcelain. It is then fired, becomes fused to the surface of the article— and the craftsman sees for the first time the actual colours he has been trying to achieve.

There are several methods of doing the job, and most of them have French names—for the same kind of reason as do many kinds of Chinese porcelain, namely, that they tended to be collected and therefore classified for the first time in France.

In the *champlevé* or 'embedded' method, you scrape out small cells or pits in the base material—or have them moulded in the original material. Then you fill them up with your enamel and fire. No doubt it was this need to cut away material, or make heavy indentations in it, and consequently the need for a thick body to work on, which accounts for the use of the *champlevé* method on base metal grounds like copper and bronze rather than gold. Celtic brooches and clasps of bronze decorated in this way and dating back 2,000 years have been unearthed in both England and France.

Another method of enamelling, called *basse taille*, has the design worked in low relief on the metal itself, and is seen through a coating of translucent coloured enamels. Yet another process which makes use of translucency for its effect is called *plique à jour*. Here the enamels are suspended in little cells made from wires: the process is used mostly for jewellery.

But one of the most popular methods of enamelling metal, which also makes use of cells, or *cloisons*, is called *cloisonné*. Here the small cells are formed by soldering to the metal surface a narrow band of copper, silver or gold which follows the lines of the decoration and separates one coloured enamel from another.

Before the enamel is filled in, these *cloisons* form a kind of map on the surface, an elaborate trellis work into which moistened powdered enamel is poured. Originally these pieces were fired in an open courtyard, using a charcoal fire fanned by a group of men standing around the brazier. A number of firings were needed to fill the *cloisons*, and the hard enamel was then polished with pumice stone, while the top edge of the metal wires forming the *cloisons* had to be gilded, as had any copper left uncovered, for example that on the base.

The Chinese are usually credited with having invented everything under the sun, but in fact this kind of enamelling was introduced there from elsewhere in Asia or perhaps Constantinople in early Ming times, i.e. in about the fourteenth century. But when they did pick up the idea— they called it *kuei kuo yao* or 'ware of the devil's country'— they made original and brilliant use of it.

Ming enamels have strikingly brilliant and pure colours, but they are so rare that most collectors have to content themselves with the wares of the later Ch'ing emperors. Nevertheless, the Ch'ing dynasty includes K'ang Hsi (1662–1722), and anyone acquainted with the marvellous porcelains produced in China during the reign of this powerful and cultured monarch will expect to find the same high quality in the enamels made at the same time.

For these and other manufactures he collected skilled craftsmen from all over China and set up more than thirty factories in the Forbidden City of Peking itself. There were metal foundries and glass works, there were the establishments of workers in jade, gold and filigree, wood engraving

Canton enamel snuffbox of copper gilt painted with a group of Europeans, two of them shooting with bows and arrows at a basket on a pole. Inside is a European river landscape. (Sotheby & Co.)

and ivory carving, lacquer making and jewellery mounting. There were workshops making lanterns, painted boxes, sceptres, artificial flowers, incense-burning sets, helmets and armour, even producing clocks, watches and optical instruments. All this in the year 1680!

Cloisonné enamels were an important part of the operations. K'ang Hsi enamels still have a good deal of the simple broad treatment, rich colours and vigorous design of the Ming work; and in the succeeding reign, that of Ch'ien Lung, there was even an improvement in the technical quality of the work. But generally speaking nothing subsequently approached these high standards.

CH'IEN LUNG CASKETS

Among all the incense burners in the form of mythical monsters, ritual vases, wine pots, altar-pieces and the rest, we shall find some fine boxes. In the Victoria and Albert Museum there is a little casket bearing the six-character mark of the reign of Ch'ien Lung which, interestingly enough, is decorated in the style of Ming fifteenth-century work. The wires are not of copper, but of a soft yellowish metal which may be gold: it has finely cast gilt-bronze lion-handles and the finial is of the same material.

Another of the large boxes in the same place and from about the same times is one in *repoussé* work, introduced into

(Above) *Mughal jade box and tray*. (Victoria & Albert Museum.)
(Below) *Chinese dark green jade incense burner*, $4\frac{9}{16}$ *ins. high*. (Sotheby & Co.)

China about this time. It is made with ten lobes decorated with flower sprays in a single enamel colour, a dark cobalt blue, the copper base being gilded in exposed places. There are also examples of work in *champlevé*, often on a base of silver or silver foil which has been etched or engraved and covered with transparent enamels.

Marks have been mentioned: in Ming times they are complicated and often very misleading, but in the Ch'ing Dynasty these seem to be almost exclusive to pieces made in the reign of Ch'ien Lung. Most of them are incised or carved, perhaps on a rectangular panel set in the piece, but a few are moulded. Sometimes there are four characters in a double-lined square, sometimes four or six characters with a 'mark of commendation' below similar to those found on Chinese porcelain; or the piece may be marked *yu*, for jade, meaning that in the marker's view it is worthy of comparison with the most beloved of the Chinese connoisseur's materials.

Japanese *cloisonné* enamel of the early and mid nineteenth century, once avidly collected but now rather looked down upon for its crowded decoration, suffers very much from the lack of the fine turquoise colour which is such an outstanding feature of Chinese work. But there is some work from the later nineteenth century which is very collectable. There is great variety in the colours, and fine craftsmanship in the application of the wires. Decoration is restrained and often taken from growing plants, or landscapes with birds, flowers and butterflies in naturalistic styles. It is all rather reminiscent of *Art Nouveau* themes, and at the same time some of the more naturalistic decorative ideas used in Victorian pottery of the better sorts; and in fact the appearance is much more of painted enamels than of the *cloisonné* technique. This school of enamel workers was led by Namikawa Yasuyuki of Kyoto.

PAINTED ENAMELS

We have been looking at enamel work which was used in the same kind of way as a precious stone is put in a setting: it is more than likely that this was how *cloisonné* actually originated.

Now we come to the very much wider field of enamels used for painting or printing. The idea first arose in Venice in the fifteenth century, where the process was used in decorating glass. From here it spread, naturally enough, to the glassmakers of Limoges, who produced an opaque white enamel with the same oxide of tin used for faience or maiolica.

Covering a surface with this opaque white they would then paint a picture in black which not only looked like the woodcuts in the new printed books but often took its subject from them.

On this foundation the enamellers then laid enamels of different colours—usually brown or blue—in the form of a moist powder, using either a brush or a spatula, until they had something like a picture in very fine sand.

Today we admire the restraint of the Limoges enamels, but this was, in fact, dictated by the difficulty of getting a wide enough range of colours which would stand up to the requirements of painting on metal and firing at high temperatures. The enamellers were short of pinks for flesh tints, and had to use manganese; this gave the characteristic violet tone of faces on the early Limoges enamels. But their cobalt blue was splendid, and there was a good turquoise from copper and browns of several tints. By the time they had pointed up their highlights by stippling with gold leaf and covering their skies with golden stars, there could hardly be anything more colourful.

Perhaps the best-known style of Limoges, however, is the painting *en grisaille*, that is to say, in a series of greys, and this has since been revived, notably in the late nineteenth century.

FAMILLE ROSE ENAMELS

We left China with *cloisonné* and *champlevé* enamels. We now go back there to see what they may have done about painted enamels. Once again, the process is called not only 'foreign' but *yang tz'u*, that is, 'foreign porcelain'—the Chinese never really took anything seriously but jade and porcelain.

(Below left) *Copper gilt reliquary engraved with* champlevé *enamel; the lid shows St George overcoming the Dragon.* (Victoria & Albert Museum.)

(Right) *Copper gilt with* champlevé *enamel pyx, for carrying the consecrated host. Limoges, thirteenth century, height $4\frac{3}{8}$ ins.* (Victoria & Albert Museum.)

During the reign of Louis XIV, contemporary of the Chinese Emperor K'ang Hsi, French and English families ordered table services in enamels which—like the famous porcelain misleadingly known in the West as Armorial Lowestoft—bore their coats of arms and crests. Both, in fact, were decorated in the same shops, and there are examples where, say, a teapot is enamelled on copper and the rest of the service on porcelain.

But the great attraction of these K'ang Hsi enamels is the way they display the *famille rose* colours and motifs already mentioned, with brocaded patterns and diapered bands and the usual foliated panels. Boxes in this ware are among the most colourful items one can find.

EUROPEAN ENAMELS

Among European painted enamels, eighteenth-century France once again takes the lead, especially Paris. Glance through a collection of boxes of this era and you will find the most exquisite blending of colours in the patterned enamels, renderings of flowers and stars, imitations of the striations of natural stones, or unbroken grounds of rich colours.

Unsurpassed in their kind, too, are the boxes with panels painted either with the portrait miniatures already mentioned, *paysages*, or rural scenes, general pictures showing the daily life and work of the times, and classical scenes. Here ladies and gentlemen recline against tree-stumps in gardens, singing from music books or playing with mandolines. Girls dance before gentleman fiddlers sitting on rocks, sportsmen set out with setters, shepherds seek to embrace shepherdesses while elderly women wring their hands in the background. Venuses chide Cupids or mourn Adonises, there are harlequinades, Bacchic revelries, military parades, naval battles, ruins, majestic vistas. Many of these subjects are from originals by court painters like Watteau, Boucher or Fragonard, by masters of still life like Chardin, of *genre* like Teniers. Some are the artist-enamellers' own original work, like that of Jean Petitot, one of the most famous of them.

Battersea or Bilston enamels. (From top) *Needlecase with tulip top; pugdog's head snuffbox; étui or scissors case; shoe snuffbox.*

28

BATTERSEA OR BILSTON?

For English and American collectors we have now reached the age—and also the problem—of Battersea. What exactly is a 'Battersea Box'? At one time there was no difficulty in answering this question. Any small box of the eighteenth century, printed or painted on enamel, was considered to be from Battersea, and that was all about it.

But facts have now come to light which seem to prove that very, very few of the enamels credited to Battersea were ever made there. A few years ago the late Mr W. B. Honey searched in the Battersea rate books and discovered that in the middle of 1753 York House, where the enamels were made, was marked as 'empty'. Three years later, the following sale was publicly announced:

'To be sold by auction, by order of the assignees, on Monday next, June 8. 1756, and the following days, at York Place, at Battersea, in Surrey—The

Battersea or Bilston enamels. (From top) *Human head snuffboxes; dolphin's head snuffbox; goldfinch snuffbox.*

29

(Left) Bonbonnière *in form of basket, chased gilt metal with enamel lid painted at Battersea, diameter $2\frac{3}{8}$ ins.* (Victoria & Albert Museum.)

(Below right) *Staffordshire enamel tea caddy painted in colours and gold. $4\frac{1}{8}$ ins. high.* (Victoria & Albert Museum.)

Household furniture and entire stock of Stephen Theodore Janssen, Esq., consisting of a great variety of beautiful enamell'd pictures, snuffboxes, watch-cases, bottle tickets, etc.; great variety of black enamels of various sizes, copper frames for mounting the unfinished enamels, with all the utensils, etc., belonging to the manufactory, also a great number of copper plates, beautifully engraved by the best hands. . . . The place is most pleasantly situated, with a convenient creek for barges and boats coming up to the houses, which has been fitted up at a very great expense, with every conveniency for carrying on the said manufactory which, if any person think of continuing, they may be treated with by the assignees before the date of sale.'

Nobody did think of continuing 'the said manufactory'—at least there is no record of anyone having done so—and with the bankruptcy of Stephen Theodore Janssen, a former Lord Mayor of London, occasioned by the disastrous South Sea Bubble, the brief three years' existence of the Battersea enamel factory came to an end.

MORE BILSTON THAN BATTERSEA

Obviously no more than a tithe of the enamels normally credited to Battersea could possibly have been made there in such a short time. But there are many other reasons for believing that the great majority of those in our collections were actually made at Bilston and other places in South Staffordshire. It was not far from the North Staffordshire potteries, where skilled painters were to be found, nor from Birmingham, where the metal frames of the boxes were made. On the evidence of style alone, many boxes must have been made long after the Battersea factory closed, and we know that French enamellers and a thriving industry in 'toys' of this sort flourished around Birmingham even earlier in the century than Battersea. It is now almost taken for granted, moreover, that even with the actual products of York House, the 'blanks'—metal mounts and enamel grounds—were imported from Bilston and only painted or printed at Battersea.

Some of them, indeed, may have been so treated elsewhere in London. Sometimes one comes across a porcelain box with an enamelled copper lid, such as a certain *bonbonnière* in the Schreiber Collection. This is obviously of Chelsea porcelain—this factory opened·a few years before the York House venture—and equally obviously the lid is in one of the styles which do not occur *after* the closing of Battersea, but *does* occur on Chelsea porcelain after that date. It has therefore been asked if these porcelain boxes may not have been bought by someone who also bought the lids from the enamellers—the lids would have had to be fitted to the boxes rather than vice versa because of the way porcelain shrinks in the kiln.

That someone may very well have been one of the outside decorators—equivalent to the German *hausmalerei* or home decorators who bought plain porcelain and glass and painted them in their studios. This kind of work also went on in the back rooms of the 'jewellers' who sold these precious trifles, as is noted in another book in this series dealing with Bristol Glass.

In fact, there is an interesting little round box painted with flowers on a dark blue enamel ground in the Victoria and Albert Museum which—it has been demonstrated by Sir Herbert Read—was undoubtedly painted by the same hand and in the same palette as some blue glass enamelled bottles which until now have been considered to be of Bristol make. Nobody has ever claimed that enamel boxes were painted in Bristol, and it may be that both box and glass were painted in either London or the Midlands; furthermore a correspondence between the decoration of another box at South Kensington and that of a watch-case made in London by Richard Hampton seems to point to a London—but post-Battersea—origin for both. Another box too late for Battersea bears the mark 'Made by Anth. Tregent in Regent Street', which suggests that Bilston may well have supplied the blanks to other places than Battersea.

SOME BATTERSEA STYLES

Mr Rackham, in the catalogue of the Schreiber Collection, awards to Battersea a number of groups at the Victoria and Albert Museum. First there are the snuffboxes and other items with painting in colours which have the same mannerisms—such as a rendering of clouds with ragged touches of blue—as the painter of the famous Aesop's Fables subjects on Chelsea porcelain. In some cases the painting is based on a well-known print.

There are also some larger boxes in the Schreiber Collection which appear—although in a different style—to be by the same hand. One is a casket with an Italian landscape subject based on themes from the French painter François Boucher: the sides and bottom are decorated with small bouquets and detached sprays of flowers. Another casket shows in colours two scenes from pictures by another famous French court painter, Antoine Watteau—while inside the box is a copy of a third picture, the well-known subject *Pensent-ils au raisin?* (see colour plate), where a shepherdess offers fruit to a young shepherd who is obviously thinking of nothing of the sort. A third box in this class shows a lady and gentleman in the costume of about 1750 sitting on the ground with an open music book between them listening to a flute player. Other Battersea styles were adopted in the Staffordshire workshops, but not this one.

COLOURS AND GROUNDS

Other criteria for genuine Battersea offered by Mr Honey are the grounds and certain of the colours used in the painting. There is one quite distinctive type of ground, thick and of a warm white colour and brilliant surface like soft-paste porcelain, for which it can easily be mistaken. On both this and the colder white surface of other pieces, the Battersea colours melted with what Mr Honey described as a charmingly 'wet' translucent effect, entirely different from the opaque gouache effect of the later work. He also draws attention to three colours peculiar to Battersea: a deep bright crimson, a clear bright blue and especially a warm reddish dark brown.

TRANSFER PRINTING ON ENAMELS

But the most striking known work at Battersea and an innovation there was printing on enamels, an art which afterwards spread to porcelain and which can truly be claimed as an English (or perhaps one should say Irish) invention.

Stephen Janssen was himself a stationer, and so would have been thoroughly conversant with the techniques of making prints. His partners, or perhaps employees, included Henry Delamain, a Dublin delftware maker, and John Brooks, an Irish engraver, and it is the latter who is generally credited with the development of transfer printing on copper. This is done in much the same fashion as children do their 'colour transfers'—an impression is taken on paper in ink from a copper plate and this, while still damp, can be transferred to any suitable material.

33

At Battersea, the engraving was extremely fine, but seems to have needed additional decoration by hand, with soft washes of transparent colours over the printing in black, brown, brick-red, mauve or crimson. The very individual fluent line of Simon-François Ravenet, a skilful French engraver, is a hallmark of Battersea, as is also some work which appears to be by the hand of that Robert Hancock who afterwards introduced transfer printing to Worcester. In the same kind of way, typically French motifs such as those taken from the works of the court painters Watteau

Caddy or 'tea-box' of Dresden (Meissen) porcelain, with brilliantly painted landscapes in reserved panels on a turquoise ground. Said to have been presented by the King of Saxony to the Empress Elizabeth of Russia. (Sotheby & Co.)

and Boucher, but now engraved rather than painted, are characteristic of the short-lived York House establishment.

BILSTON'S COLOURED GROUNDS

Battersea, on the whole, seemed to like white backgrounds. When we turn to Bilston, we come across a range of coloured backgrounds, and as the enamellers undoubtedly derived a lot of their ideas from Chelsea porcelain, the sequence of the appearance of coloured grounds used there may be a useful guide in dating the enamels. Mr Rackham gives dark blue as a ground colour in use from 1755, pea-green from 1757, turquoise and claret from 1760 and silver, yellow and a golden red from 1770.

Other colours on the Bilston enamels are the typically English lavender blue, plum and a brownish olive. Pink, that very popular colour at Sèvres—where it was called *rose pompadour*—did not get here until 1770, which puts Battersea out of court for it. It is sometimes referred to as *rose dubarry*—anachronistically, for the lady referred to did not rise to Royal favour until a generation after the Pompadour. Many boxes with this ground were sent abroad, where it was known as 'English Pink'.

Bilston may well have absorbed craftsmen thrown out of work by the closing-down of Battersea. In one case there is evidence of a Battersea style—with characteristically dark thunderclouds in lilac and dove grey—appearing on a piece which was obviously too late to have been made on Thames-side. Another Bilston painter used landscapes with a

35

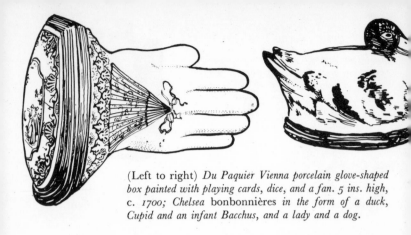

(Left to right) *Du Paquier Vienna porcelain glove-shaped box painted with playing cards, dice, and a fan. 5 ins. high, c. 1700;* Chelsea *bonbonnières in the form of a duck, Cupid and an infant Bacchus, and a lady and a dog.*

heavy chocolate brown and interiors with a heavy grey slate colour or lavender as a background. Yet another liked to do pleasant little scenes in a rather naïve manner of families walking in a garden or by a river, or being pushed on swings.

ALMANAC BOXES

Dating themselves more helpfully than most pieces are those snuff boxes printed with almanacs, usually headed 'A New Year's Gift for 1758', or whatever year it was, and giving the fixed and movable feasts, eclipses of the sun and moon, etc.

Pieces can be dated in other ways. For example there is an *étui* painted with a portrait of Catherine Chambers, wife of the architect Sir William Chambers, which was taken from an engraving made in 1756. So also with a little writing box, fitted with a square inkpot and pounce pot, a faceted circular wafer box all of cut glass with enamelled caps mounted in gilt metal and a seal of green glass with an intaglio classical head, and two pens and a combined pen and pencil holder of gilt metal. The printed decoration shows groups of women with baskets and birds which are taken from a series of engravings symbolizing the twelve months, by P. C. Canot, published in London in 1759.

BIRD AND ANIMAL SHAPES

One of the most fascinating types of little enamel boxes comes in the shape of birds, animals, human heads and so on. The Battersea enamellers seem to have picked up the idea from Chelsea—or perhaps from Chelsea's source, Dresden—and the Bilston men who went there from Battersea.

This kind of anthropomorphism—if pompous words like that can be used in connection with such engaging trifles—has fascinated mankind from the days of the Incas, with their saddle bottles in human form, down to Staffordshire chimney backs or even the latest Doulton Toby jug. Here, in enamel, the eighteenth-century lady or gentleman could choose between the head of a queen, wearing a gold crown lined with crimson and crossed by jewelled gilt bows with blue fleurs-de-lis, and a dragon, printed in purple and painted in colours, or a naked Negro boy caressing a tiger and feeding him with grapes.

Heads of dolphins, lions, boars, and dogs of various kinds, especially the beloved pugdog of the day, find themselves at home in collectors' cases alongside parrots, swans, woodcocks, finches and pairs of billing doves. There is one shaped for an eagle fighting with a cat; on its lid is a print, painted over, of a cat throttling an eagle, which is flying in mid-air with the cat in its claws: one wonders who thought of such a subject and still more who would want to buy it. Some of these items are shown on pages 28–9.

FRUIT AND FLOWERS

A series of *bonbonnières* thought to be of Battersea make take the forms of fruits and flowers. Here you may choose between an egg, quite plain white, and various fruits in natural colours, including peaches, apples, lemons, and walnuts. There is one very pretty one in the form of a red rose, with green leaves and stalk and a spray of flowers painted inside the lid. In the eighteenth century the shell motif was never far away, whether in the mid-century rococo forms or in the later Adam styles, so one will not be surprised to find among these enamels *bonbonnières* in the form of cowrie shells decorated with nymphs and cupids after Boucher.

Scottish collectors will note with approval that highlanders are shown—in one the gentleman is embracing a shepherdess, his bagpipes thrown down carelessly among the sheep. On the other hand Irish collectors will perhaps not be very enthusiastic about a snuffbox with a portrait of that Duke of Dorset who was Lord Lieutenant of Ireland from 1751 to 1755, which carries an allegorical print of Britannia encouraging Irish manufactures, as symbolized by Hibernia with a distaff and a loom.

Shoes were always very popular for snuffboxes of all kinds. They may be in white enamel with the pointed toe and high heel of the period (of any period) decorated with bouquets and detached flowers, the heel in crimson and the stitching, buckle and strap in lines of yellow edged with red.

Enamel was sometimes combined with chased silver in these snuffboxes. There is one which is a silver box, the sides of which are chased with rococo scrollwork and the bottom of mother-of-pearl engraved with a large rosette. The lid is of enamel printed in red and painted in colours with a bouquet and a butterfly.

If ever a box labelled itself as genuine Battersea it is the one in the Victoria and Albert Museum which commemorates the 'Free British Fishery Society', for Stephen Theodore Janssen played an important part in this organization, which was founded in 1750. This one shows a gentleman, presumed to be that Frederick Prince of Wales who did not survive his father George II and so failed to give us our first King Fred: with a lady he is watching three men putting fish in kegs, to the dismay of two Dutch fishermen; a ribbon wishes 'Success to the British Fishery'.

SONGS AND MOTTOES

Some boxes carry inscriptions in French—a sign that they were made either for export or to titillate the vanity of the ladies and gentlemen of St James.

Messages like '*A la chasse amoureuse*' on a hunting scene leave no doubt of their real significance; neither do '*Inflexible en amour c'est folie*' or '*Larmes d'amour*'.

There were songs, together with music. Here is one called 'Ariette':

> *Toujours le Zephir*
> *Plus gay qui fidelle*
> *Des fleurs a choisir*
> *Prend la plus nouvelle,*
> *Et de belle en belle*
> *Vole a son desir.*

On the bottom of the same snuffbox is another song entitled 'Fanfare'. It runs:

> *Colin toute la nuit*
> *Veille en songeant a Catin*
> *Et pour Collin elle a la puce*
> *A Loreille du soir jusqu'au matin*
> *Un grand Medecin a dit*
> *Qu'on les couche en un meme lit*
> *La puce en denichera,*
> *Colin alors dormira.*

39

I will leave to the reader the pleasure of translating the somewhat erratic French of these verses.

ENAMEL TOBACCO BOXES

Tobacco smokers as well as snufftakers were catered for by the enamellers, their boxes usually measuring something like $4\frac{3}{4}$ ins. by $1\frac{3}{4}$ ins. high by $2\frac{1}{4}$ ins. Subjects, as one might antici-pate, cover such activities as stag and boar hunting, fowling, haymaking and convivial scenes in Dutch inns, but there are still ladies and gentlemen in gardens, and bouquets of flowers.

Frederick the Great of Prussia, then revered in this country as an ally against the French, is commemorated here as on porcelain and pottery of the time, as is John Wilkes.

NINETEENTH-CENTURY ENAMELS

Enamels a long way inferior to the early ones poured out from Staffordshire from 1780 onwards, deteriorating steadily as the nineteenth century grew. But in spite of less exquisite workmanship many of them have great charm as period pieces. They still commemorate events, proclaim themselves as 'Trifles from' London, Worcester, Margate or wherever it is: sometimes they bear the name of a shop which gave them to favoured customers. Mottoes were no longer in the French mode: one sees more often 'Trifles Show Respect' and 'Live and Let Live', than which there could hardly be anything more phlegmatically British. But 'Within you see what pleases me' reminds one that the early mirrors of steel now began to be replaced by glass.

The enamellers met their Waterloo, as Napoleon did his, in the Napoleonic wars, when their flourishing export trade was suddenly cut off, and the cost of copper soared. But at least one enameller went on, for Samuel Yardley of Wednesbury continued in business until 1840. But by late Victorian days, so little was thought of painted enamels that—according to Mr Bernard Hughes—when his son, John Yardley, died, several clothes baskets full of his enamels went to a dealer for a few shillings.

4. English Silver

English collectors are not normally great collectors of gold boxes—who is?—being more at home, and less likely to starve their families, with the many interesting boxes which are to be found in less precious materials.

For example, sterling silver. The early tobacco boxes, stately and refined productions, date from about the 1660s. Some have richly worked renaissance designs, but surprisingly many are quite plain, except for a coat of arms.

Once snuff had got under way, the English silversmith showed his usual sense of craftsmanship and style in making boxes for it. The early ones are small and slender, engraved, embossed or chased, and there are more oval ones than later. Not unexpectedly, many have sporting themes, especially the large table ones which were set out when company was about. There is a good deal of gilding—the insides were always gilt, of course, to protect the silver from the action of the snuff and its flavourings. The *niello* process, whereby lines cut in the design are filled with a black substance, was also very effectively used. High relief work is to be found on the boxes of the early nineteenth century.

Apart from solid silver boxes, there are many types where silver is used in combination with some other material. Shells and semi-precious stones were brought into use and

Charles I commemoration silver snuffbox. The English inscription runs 'Thee, Glorious Martyr, Rebells did destroy, they, God, who was Their aim, Could not anoy. Carolus Primus Rex Martyrio Coronatus Jan 30: 1648.' It also bears the arms of the Wight family. Hallmarked, apparently, for 1713. (Sotheby & Co.)

41

mounted with silver, or the box might be of solid silver and the cover of mounted ivory. In other versions the box itself was made of some hardstone like agate and then enclosed in chased silver openwork, thus enabling the design of foliage, birds and flowers to stand out engagingly against the background of the stone used.

SCENTS AND SPICES

Perhaps the smallest kind of silver box—sometimes no larger than a postage stamp—is the vinaigrette. They have a fretted grille inside—or did once—under which a sponge soaked in aromatic 'vinegars' was kept to assist in fainting fits or to overcome bad smells. They came in all kinds of shapes—as books, purses, shells, acorns, nuts, barrels, strawberries, helmets, beehives, snails, watches, chests—in fact almost everything you can think of. Some of them are set with semi-precious stones, or they may be wholly of these stones and set with silver.

Predecessor of the vinaigrette was the pomander, itself a

Silver-gilt George IV table snuff box decorated in a pastoral scene in the Louis Quinze manner. (Delieb & Co.)

descendant of the *pomme d'ambre*, or apple of amber— and incidentally ancestor of the dried orange stuck with cloves which one once used to see. Some pomanders are more complicated than others, but they generally take the form of a round contrivance with up to eight segments rather like those of the orange itself; they open individually and disclose compartments filled with herbs and oils.

PLEASURES OF PIQUÉ

One can hardly leave this world of gold and silver and fine craftsmanship without mentioning one form of decoration which for many is a collecting field of its own.

The art of *piqué* gives a gold or silver inlay on boxes and other items in tortoiseshell, mother-of-pearl and ivory. Sometimes the decoration is made up of tiny points of metal, when it is called *piqué point*; *piqué clouté* uses rather larger points or 'nails' arranged in a pattern; while in *piqué posé* the silver or gold is laid on in flat cut-out shapes.

Early *piqué* of the Louis XIV period is perhaps the finest, the designs being in *'foules point d'or'*, or literally, crowds of gold point; but later on *piqué posé* was extensively used for classical groups, with decoration of fleurs de lys, flies, gnats, vine leaves, grape clusters and other subjects in *piqué point*. In the Louis XVI period, and also during the

(Left) *French snuffbox in* piqué posé *and* piqué point.
(Right) *Snuffbox in* piqué *work. English nineteenth century.*

Second Empire, the favourite symbol used in decoration is the star and a sprig pattern.

English *piqué* starts in the seventeenth century, with tobacco boxes decorated in tiny circles arranged in pyramid or other formations. But the period of perfection seems to have been from about 1740 to 1760, that is to say at the height of the rococo era. Then follow Dutch scenes (presumably influenced by the brass tobacco boxes) and chinoiseries, also some very ornate boxes in the Chippendale style. At the end of the century there is the usual Adam restraint, with honeysuckle, swags and urns, together with some shuttle-shaped boxes having cable patterns with an oval pattera, or miniature.

Regency and Victorian *piqué* is of good quality, but much heavier in treatment. About the 1870s mechanical methods made it possible to stamp out the decorations.

Piqué work is also to be found on bone, wood, shagreen, marble, agate and various artificial compositions.

What is found in silver is usually also to be found in Sheffield plate. Styles and types are similar, so perhaps it will be enough simply to indicate, for the benefit of those who don't happen to know, what exactly Sheffield plate is.

In effect it is a method of making a little silver go a long way. A thin sheet of pure silver is fused on to a thick slab of copper; this slab is then rolled out thinly into sheets and worked up in the same way as sterling silver itself—with a few modifications. The story goes that the process was discovered about the year 1750 by a metalworker named Boulsover, who was repairing a piece of silver, and used a copper coin to wedge it in a vice; on applying heat he found he had fused the two metals. Buttons and then snuffboxes were among the first of Boulsover's productions.

Before then, and for a few years in the early nineteenth century, the same kind of effect had been achieved by what was known as close-plating, whereby the piece was first made up in the base metal, and a thin layer of silver soldered on afterwards.

One thing you can be sure of is that if the word 'Sheffield' appears on a piece with or without a number, it is not Sheffield plate at all, but Britannia metal, a kind of pewter. Sometimes this is electro-plated, when the initial letters E.P.B.M.—electro-plated Britannia metal—may appear. Similarly E.P.N.S. means electro-plated nickel silver—in other words ordinary electro-plated.

(Top left to top right) *Silver pomander, English seventeenth century. Vinaigrettes in the form of a heart, an articulated fish, a walnut, a book, a handbag, and an acorn.*

45

5. Oriental Lacquer

Not in the finest goldsmith's work of eighteenth-century Paris, not in the richest enamels of Limoges, the most sophisticated porcelains of Meissen or the shining silvers of London is there to be found any more subtlety of subject and design than in the works of the Japanese lacquer artists. Nor is there to be found such astonishing virtuosity with materials which the craftsmen of the West would have thought unworthy of such painstaking labour.

On the many kinds of boxes made of lacquer and the materials associated with it—gold and silver, but also wood, paper, shells, pewter, coral, even hempen cloth—you will find beautifully judged decoration of all the subjects beloved of the Japanese—the plant's tendril, clouds and mountains, birds or beasts in action, human beings faced with their real or imagined worlds. Here are legendary monsters, gods and goddesses, scholars and lovers, wind and snow, the fury of fighting and the tranquillity of gardens.

Here, in fact, is the Japanese love of the 'thing which exists' in picture poems, in which every line tells its story. Shinto priests cross rivers in procession; mandarin ducks sit on rocks by streams; the pine, bamboo and plum (the 'three friends') offer you long life, rectitude and sweetness. Peacocks, tortoises, cherry blossom, butterflies, birds of paradise, doves, peonies and nightingales, all convey their special significance—like the *ho ho* bird who brings good fortune when it comes to earth. So, too, do autumn moons, princes in travelling carriages, cranes in water reeds, ladies writing of their loves on screens. Somewhere in all these motifs you will find traces of all the cultural streams which have flowed into Japanese art and been given a new life of their own.

46

The boxes themselves are, as in most countries, used for tobacco, cosmetics, medicine and the like; but also for such special purposes as the Poem Card Game, the Incense Ceremony, or the Tea Ceremony.

The Poem Card Game was originally a shell game, whereby twenty or thirty specially beautiful shells made a pack which was kept in a circular box, and players had to match the two halves of a bivalve. A later refinement in showing the affinity of two shells was achieved by inscribing the two halves of a famous couplet. When the Portuguese introduced card-playing, the ladies used them, not for playing the Western games, but for writing the matching halves of their poems. In the Tea Ceremony—something between a social occasion and a religious rite—not only were there cabinets for tea utensils like bowls, whisks and tea boxes, but also counters and scoreboard, for drawing lots for precedence in the ceremony.

Some of the best lacquer boxes were made for the Incense Ceremony or contest, in which participants had to guess the type of incense passed round in bundles and then use some allusively poetic name to describe it. The boxes held censer, miniature chopping blocks, knives, tongs, spatulas, instrument stands and marking boards for the score. Very large sums were paid for these sets. There were also picnic boxes, for the annual or biennial excursion to take the local gods out for an airing; these held bottles and cups for *saké*—the national drink made from rice—dishes or trays and boxes for the foodstuffs.

LACQUER PROCESSES

But so far we have not talked about lacquer itself. What exactly is it?

Confusion surrounds the word because it has been used rather indiscriminately to describe, first, the work of the Far East which we are now considering; secondly, Burmese lac, which is the gummy deposit of an insect; and thirdly,

47

(Top) *Japanese Incense Ceremony cabinet with views in* takamakije *of gold and silver,* kirikane, hirame, nashije *and gold and silver foil on black* (ro-iro). *Early nineteenth century.* $9\frac{1}{2} \times 10\frac{3}{4} \times 6\frac{1}{2}$ ins. (Victoria & Albert Museum.)

(Middle) *Picnic case in* nashiji *lacquer painted in gold. Nineteenth century.* (Victoria & Albert Museum.)

(Bottom) *Sweetmeat box in form of a butterfly.* (Victoria & Albert Museum.)

(Left) *Toad tobacco box with a wooden pipe case made as a snake coiled round a toad.* (Victoria & Albert Museum.)

(Right) *Japanese inro of four cases, with a three-tailed goldfish in coloured togidashi among waterweeds and waves. Signed 'Shunsho' with red seal and complete with coral bead and gold lacquer manju with a goldfish in colours in applied horn.* (Sotheby & Co.)

those artificial concoctions from resins and gums which have been and still are being used in the West for what is usually called 'japanning'.

True lac is a remarkable material, for unlike most others it improves, or at any rate hardens, with dampness. The ship bringing home the Japanese exhibits from the Vienna exhibition of 1878—doubtless one of those which helped to set the wave of enthusiasm for Japanese art in the West—ran herself upon a reef and foundered; but when the cargo was recovered some months later the lacquer ware was found to be quite unharmed.

Lacquer can be ground with whetstone to whatever degree of fineness you require, and after polishing with burnt clay, horn ashes or the like, can be given a more brilliant sheen even than glazed pottery, silver or enamel. Its only real enemy, in fact, is bright light, which can make it fade and even decompose.

FORMS OF DECORATION

But more remarkable than the material itself, perhaps, is the diversity and ingenuity of the processes used in making and decorating articles of lacquer. The basis of most pieces is wood, usually pine of a soft and even grain, worked very thin in the smaller pieces. Upon this may be gummed layers of tough paper, hemp cloth, plaited bamboo hide or the like, and a fine piece may call for twenty or thirty processes.

In the better salerooms, the pieces are classified according to the chief process used; and I have summarized these from the classifications made by Lt.-Col. E. F. Strange in the catalogue of the collection in the Victoria and Albert Museum, London, which contains some of the best anywhere.

In *chinkin-bori* a hairline design is engraved upon a lacquer surface with a pin, and gold leaf worked into the design so made; *fundame* gives a matt finish with fine gold or silver powder. In *guri* coloured lacquers are used in successive layers, and a simple scroll design is cut through them— in V-shaped section—to show the edges of the different colours. *Hakeme* indicates that the brush mark may clearly be seen and imitates the grain of wood. *Hiramaki-e* shows decoration in low relief, built up with lacquer, while *hirame* has irregular pieces of sheet gold or silver set out on the surface.

Kamakura-bori, one of the most popular processes, has a design engraved or carved in wood, and lacquered in different colours. Cinnabar and green will be used in layers to give the effect of red flowers and green leaves. *Kinji* has a ground covered with gold lacquer, while *kirikane* is a

Leaden box covered with carved cinnabar lacquer. Diameter 3⅖ ins. Eighteenth century. (Victoria & Albert Museum.)

mosaic-like process, whereby rectangles of sheet gold or silver are inlaid in the lacquer.

Nashiji reminds one of aventurine glass, with its random flecks of gold and silver 'adventuring' where it will. The trick is done in lacquer by placing the small flakes of metal between various layers of lac, so that they seem to be floating at different levels, as if imprisoned in ice.

Raden—one of the most popular and delightful of the techniques—uses inlaid shell in combination with metals such as gold, silver and pewter. The nautilus shell, so well known in Western crafts, is used here; also green and blue iridescent shells like the awabi, or 'sea-ear'. The lacquer is usually applied on a base of red sandalwood or other hardwood, and after the cut-out designs have been mounted on the base, the whole is coated over with lacquer and polished; the lacquer film on the surface may be scraped off with a knife to bring up the design.

Roiro-nuri is highly polished black lacquer sometimes involving as many as twenty-eight processes. It has been much used in the Japanese Tea Ceremony, a fashion for black utensils having been set by a famous Master in the later sixteenth century.

51

Ko-ju-bako, *or one of a set of boxes for the Japanese Incense Ceremony. Covered with herons in a stream in* takamakiye *of gold and silver enriched with* kirikane *on* fundame *ground*. (Victoria & Albert Museum.)

Sabiji is itself an interesting expression; it describes a feeling for the qualities of anything which is old or tarnished, or rough in texture, or perhaps unfinished; the implication is that the thing is sincere and not artificial. *Sabi* finds expression in much of the coarse pottery used, for example, in the Tea Ceremony; and of course nowadays is also to be found in the sculpture and pottery of the West.

Makie is one of the main types of decoration, whereby a design is drawn in lacquer and gold or silver studs strewn over it. In *hira-makie* there is no foundation and decoration in low relief is built up in the lacquer; with *taka-makie* there is high relief, built up with various substances in combination with lacquer, and then coated and further enriched in various ways. *Togidashi* is the process whereby the design is drawn with gold or silver dust in slightly wet lacquer, then covered by successive layers of lacquer which are rubbed down to reveal the design richly in the flat.

Tsuguri-nuri and *Wakasa-nuri* remind one of the agate and other mottled pottery wares of Whieldon and other Staffordshire men. Lacquers of mixed colours (and in the case of *wakasa-nuri* of black, white, gold and silver) are overlaid and ground down to give interesting 'random' patterns. It is said that some is akin to our 'end-of-day' glass ware, in that it was made up from the superfluous lacquer which the artist scrapes from his brush.

Tsuishu and *Tsuikoku* are cinnamon and black carved lacquer, essentially a Chinese process, in fact the chief one, and generally showing Chinese preference for abstract rather than personalized designs. Ten layers of lacquer may be laid on successively and the design is carved in the solid mass; sometimes colours alternate and the carving makes use of this. Imitations are to be found in carved wood covered with lacquer or stamped out of composition, giving the effect of red flowers and green leaves.

INRO

But of all the boxes to be found in lacquer ware, perhaps that which most engages the curiosity and interest of the Westerner is the *inro*.

In the traditional dress of the Japanese there are no pockets, so that necessities have to be carried about the person—in the same kind of way that an eighteenth- or nineteenth-century lady carried her *étui* or scissors case and other appurtenances on a châtelaine, as described on page 8. Among the various items which hung from the girdle— tobacco box or pouch, purse, etc.—was a kind of miniature medicine chest. It consisted of a series of little boxes which fit end-on into each other and can be drawn together and closed by means of a pair of silk cords running through their sides. These two cords pass through a sliding bead, called an *ojime*, which kept them tight in the same way as in a string bag, and they end in the well-known *netsuke* or toggle which passed through the girdle and so kept all secure.

Actually these *inro* seem to have originally been used for seals, for the word appears to mean 'seal case', and some do indeed bear indications of having once carried them.

The small separate boxes of the *inro* are called cases; and

Japanese document box cover showing takamakiye *of gold, silver, shell, and pewter* (raden) *on* nashiji *lacquer. Eighteenth century.* (Victoria & Albert Museum.)

they generally number from two to seven, although there are single-case *inro* as well. Sometimes a case may be divided, or there may be a tray: it is thought that these may have been used for seals.

Inro are usually elliptical in shape, but they are also cylindrical, rectangular, hexagonal or octagonal. Occasionally they take the very logical form of a miniature cabinet, fitted with drawers, with a place for a tiny spoon to facilitate taking medicine: while a harking back to the *inro*'s ancestor may be suggested by those which are in the form of bags or pouches. It is thought that unusually large *inro*—they are commonly about $3\frac{1}{2}$ ins. by $2\frac{1}{2}$ ins. by $\frac{3}{4}$ in. deep—were used either by actors or priests.

Probably the first point which strikes the Westerner coming freshly to these items is that, no matter how ordinary the *inro*, the separate cases fit into each other perfectly; in fact if you take into consideration the extremely thin section of the wood, the quite difficult shapes used and the risks of warping in processing the piece with lacquer, this work is quite miraculous. It is difficult to think of anything in Western craftsmanship which quite compares with it.

Not all *inro* are made in lacquer ware: they may also be found—though much less frequently—in various plain woods, encrusted with metals, shell ivory and the like; in ivory itself, mother-of-pearl, tortoiseshell, various metals, and even pottery.

Inro sometimes bear signatures, but since these are in Japanese script it will not be of much help to give the names in their latinized form. Moreover, many of the artists followed the practice of most Japanese craftsmen—to be found notably in pottery—of passing on their names to their sons or favourite pupils; this may go on for a dozen generations, to the total bafflement of anyone trying to distinguish the work of the various periods. Consequently, very little is known about the individuals whose signatures are to be found, and attribution of a particular period must generally rest upon techniques and style.

6. Lead, Brass, and Pewter

Lead has seemingly been the favourite material for tobacco boxes all down the centuries since the weed first reached Europe; and indeed it is difficult to think of anything better adapted to maintain a constant temperature and humidity.

Today we tend to speak of tobacco jars, but this is to fly in the face of tradition. Those items of stoneware, earthenware and china which stand on our mantelpieces have as much right to be called a jar as a jam jar. But a receptacle for tobacco was a box, whether it was of gold, silver, enamel, pewter or whatever.

Lead tobacco boxes have a remarkable continuity of existence, from Stuart times all down through the period when the fashionable world deserted the pipe for 'nosology'. But their heyday was probably from 1750 to 1850, when they took upon themselves a great many shapes and styles of decoration. In the early ones decorative moulding was usually cast solidly with the body of the piece, but later it was applied afterwards. Some of these boxes look like tea caddies, others like the plinths of classical monuments with panels, showing, say, Leonardo's 'Last Supper'. They may bear an erstwhile owner's initials within elaborate scrolling, and often one can detect traces of painting. In the better-preserved ones these may show up as battle scenes, perhaps from the series made after the Crimean War commemorating Inkerman and Balaclava. But now that the paint has been rubbed off so many of them, possibly the chief interest is in the knob on the lid, which in itself offers a wide field for collectors. Most often seen is the Negro's head, a trade-mark long associated with tobacco, apparently being first seen here on the bales of leaf coming into the port of Bristol. But there are also heads of celebrities like Wellington and Napoleon, full figures of all kinds, serious and comic, human and animal.

The Dutch have always been great smokers and also prolific brassfounders: hence the brass tobacco boxes of very distinctive types they have been sending us for several centuries.

In those of the seventeenth century, accompanying the first wave of enthusiasm for smoking, the sides of the boxes are often of copper, with the lid in brass, stamped with all manner of designs. Most of them are pictorial, showing groups of men smoking in taverns, bear-baiting scenes, landscapes and seascapes, battles by sea and land. Some of the latter are said to come from Iserlohn, in Germany.

There are also a great many scriptural subjects, some from the Old Testament, like Jonah and the Whale and the Judgment of Solomon; but there is also one embossed on lid and bottom with ten ornamental panels illustrating the story of the Crucifixion. More worldly in their expression are those which, for example, show a man gazing at a woman and exclaiming 'Oh my beautiful mistress!'; there is another showing a couple driving in a wagon with a servant woman sitting behind, and bearing the inscription: 'Is it not good to have a cart and horses in this world?' Is it not indeed!

English brass tobacco boxes are usually less exuberant in subject, often being content with just a scroll or two, and perhaps a crest and initials. They are difficult to date: about the only way I know is by careful study of the type of metal used, which differed considerably in alloy and working down the years. There are useful specialist books which can help here.

PEWTER

Pewter, like lead, is kind to tobacco and also to snuff, and a good gathering of it finds some very collectable boxes.

There are pewter snuffboxes dating from the early eighteenth century which are substantially replicas of the silver ones of the day; but because of the softer metal the

(Above) *Lead tobacco box with Negro's head on lid.* (Farmers' Weekly Magazine Section.)
(Above right) *Brass tobacco box in the form of an owl.*
(Right) *Pewter snuffbox, the lid cast with a view of an abbey.*

decoration of engraving or chasing has sometimes worn away. Those dating from the early nineteenth century are impressed with foliate designs or views; hunting scenes were obviously very popular. Some have an inset in brass or pinchbeck, and gilding was often applied to the insides, as it was in silver boxes—although in the more recent ones this is merely gold paint. As with the lead boxes there are often traces of painting in colours on the outside. Dearest to the heart of the collector, however, are those made in the shapes of shoes, pistols, heads, cockles and other shells.

Tobacco boxes in pewter tend to follow the same kind of styles as the lead or silver ones: there are also long narrow spice boxes, token or counter boxes, sandwich cases (sometimes in combination with a flask), pounce and wafer boxes and inkstand sets for the writing desk.

A small panel of corrugated lines will betray an early match box, and this leads to another little known but very fruitful line of collecting. A whole race of metal safety boxes for matches were made from about the 1830s to the 1870s to contain the rather dangerous phosphorus matches of the day.

They came in all kinds of forms, from pillar boxes to trunks and barrels, and some had a tiny candlestick on the roof, to hold the match while one was sealing letters. Later on came the small vesta boxes to be carried on the watch chain. These too were in a great variety of shapes—animals, birds, shoes, soda siphons, fiddles, tankards and others.

Workbox in Tunbridge Ware. (Victoria & Albert Museum.)

The ancestor of the vending machine which stands outside the modern tobacconist's shop was the 'ha'penny in the slot' brass box sometimes kept in country inns, usually on the 'smoking room' table. One still hears of them coming up at sales, and one or two are even to be found in their original pubs. You put in your coin, which releases a lock and enables you to help yourself to a 'twist'. But just in case you take more than your share, there may be an inscription, something like this:

> *Gentlemen, it's for your pleasure*
> *I wait here from day to day*
> *To supply you (when at leisure)*
> *With the weed who puff must pay.*
> *For half a penny a pipeful take*
> *And pay regard to what I say.*
> *Having that, for credit's sake,*
> *Close the lid or sixpence pay.*

7. Papiermâché

Papiermâché collectors find boxes of all kinds, from the finely painted French snuffboxes of the early eighteenth century to late Victorian jewel caskets, studded with iridescent nautilus shell.

But there is papiermâché *and* papiermâché, and the observant collector will soon come to learn the differences. In the early days it was actually made of the mashed paper suggested by the title, mixed with glue, chalk and fine sand, then pressed in moulds, stoved and japanned. Papiermâché was especially favoured for snuffboxes, for the material was light and at the same time durable, it neither cracked nor warped, and it kept the snuff cool and moist better than any material except lead or pewter.

Celebrated particularly are those of what is called *vernis martin*, a kind of lac varnish, produced by the brothers Robert and Étienne Martin, who began work in Paris under Royal patronage in the 1740s. At first they copied Chinese lacquers, but later they floated their transparent varnishes over paintings of fruit, flowers and other subjects on grounds of emerald green, flecked gold and lapis lazuli. They followed these with portraits, landscapes and *genre* pictures. The secret of the composition of *vernis martin*—which was put to every conceivable use in furnishing—died with the brothers. Another variety of lacquered or japanned papiermâché was developed by Johann Heinrich Stobwasser in Berlin about 1722, and some of these show very fine painting in colours.

English papiermâché manufacturers produced many circular table snuffboxes, with fine paintings of all subjects, sometimes inside a gilt rim. Samuel Raven, a Birmingham decorator, was responsible for many of the lids, copying such well-known engravings as Wilkie's 'The Blind Fiddler',

'Rent Day', 'Village Politicians' and other popular favourites. There were portraits of the famous, religious subjects, nudes by Etty and also theatrical and sporting scenes.

From mid-Victorian days—before the final degradation of papiermâché had quite set in—there come a whole host of small boxes, and those rather charming little caskets with doors which open and reveal nests of drawers. After about 1850 the workmanship seems to deteriorate, but compensation is offered to collectors of Victoriana by the appearance about then of boxes with mottoes and jokes, sometimes even with advertisements, which at this distance of time sometimes read interestingly and amusingly.

(Right) *Powder box painted with a portrait.* (Victoria & Albert Museum.)
(Below) *Papiermâché writing box, painted and inlaid with mother-of-pearl.* (Victoria & Albert Museum.)

8. Pontypool and Usk Ware

Another kind of japanning which claims our attention is that which is done not upon papiermâché but on tin, or rather tinned iron.

This craft takes its name from the places in Wales where its manufacture originally began, although of course it is closely related to the *tôle peinte* of France and other Continental countries.

Its inventor was an Edward Allgood, who had been making tinned iron plates at Pontypool, and whose father had interested himself in working out varnishes which could be painted in fire-resistant colours. So as to preserve the secret of the process, Allgood employed only his own family, and he built up a highly successful business making all manner of things in decorated tinned iron—teapots, urns, trays, tea tables, candlesticks, caddies and also snuffboxes. These latter seem to have been greatly prized, for a contemporary purchaser complains loudly of their cost. Decoration on them often follows chinoiserie themes, but there is also flower and landscape painting. Of outstanding interest in all this ware are the splendid colours evolved for the grounds—crimson, scarlet, orange, yellow, blue and puce are among them.

When Edward Allgood died in 1763 his sons decided to part company, and one of them opened up at Usk, not far away from Pontypool, making similar wares. Eventually the manufacturers in Wolverhampton and Birmingham moved in, with painting not much inferior, if at all, to that of Pontypool and Usk.

9. Shell Ware

Ever since they have first been brought up from the bottom of the sea or picked up on the shore, shells of all shapes and iridescences have been pounced upon by craftsmen for the decoration of beautiful things. Mother-of-pearl especially has always been highly prized, and has been used to inlay or cover boxes of every imaginable kind. It comes to us as part of various shells, including the conch, but it gets its name from the fact that it is the means whereby the oyster pearl is produced, being the innermost lining of the oyster itself, and in fact of the same material as the pearl. It is because of its laminated structure that it shows its characteristic shimmering iridescence.

Where boxes—such as tea caddies, card cases, snuffboxes, etc.—are covered with mother-of-pearl, slivers of it are usually fixed on in squares or diamonds, so as to create a varied pattern of colour and iridescence. But perhaps the material shows to best advantage when it is used as an inlay or in combination with other materials, such as gold, silver, woods of various kinds, ivory, tortoiseshell and so on. There are also boxes in which the whole shell is used for the lid, and the box itself made up of cut-out strips of mother-of-pearl mounted with gold and silver framing.

10. Tunbridge Ware

'English Wood Mosaic' is an unfamiliar term, but it pretty aptly describes the wooden wares made in and around Tunbridge Wells during the late eighteenth and early nineteenth centuries. There are many boxes of this kind around—indeed there seem to be more boxes in the ware than anything else, although you will also find in it all manner of things from toys to tables.

Tunbridge ware is essentially a kind of marquetry, a patterned veneer laid upon the 'carcase' of a box. But it differs from conventional marquetry in that the veneer is made up of the ends of slips of wood, each about six inches long and about as thick as a match. To make a design—and this could be a flowering spray or even a landscape— thousands of these little slips were glued together in blocks, so that their different colours or shades made a picture at the end of the block. These blocks were then sawn across their ends so as to provide sheets of veneer: as with seaside rock, the pattern showed 'all through'. This veneer was then used as in conventional marquetry.

About 150 different woods were used, English and foreign, but no colouring matter was employed except in so far as staining effects were obtained by soaking the woods in water from the local springs. Green was a highly desired colour and was obtained by selecting oak which, though sound, had been attacked by a certain kind of fungus.

There are all kinds of these boxes, from long ones for gloves down to tiny ones for pins. The flower and bird designs are sometimes very handsome, but the chief motives are the views of places around this Kentish spa.

11. Various and Curious

Sandalwood lends itself to the most elaborate and intricate carving, and some extraordinarily detailed work is to be found in the work of the craftsmen of India, especially around Mysore. But styles throughout the country differ, sometimes the emphasis being on floral work, sometimes mythological scenes and characters being featured. The darker the colour of the wood, the better quality the piece is said to be. But the art is dying out, and anyone interested in the fine work of these village craftsmen should buy their pieces while they may.

Beadwork has been used for centuries to decorate boxes, as all manner of other things; but stumpwork is now a thing of the past. This work takes its name from the 'stump' of hair or wool used to fill out the padded parts of the design, which stand up in relief, sometimes swinging out from the piece— as in the box shown on page 66. Most of the subjects cover biblical scenes or perhaps the Stuart kings and queens which date them. All is done with an engaging naïveté, every bit of space being filled for example with birds, flowers or unicorns, interspersed with seed pearls, silver, and gilt thread and other things.

What other kinds of boxes are there to offer the curious collector?

Some of the oddest are those made from coquilla nuts. These are about the size of hens' eggs and they come from the South American piassaba plant. Carved into snuffboxes, pomanders, wafer boxes or nutmeg graters, they have sometimes been mounted in silver in Europe. Some of the early ones show biblical subjects, but from early in the nineteenth century there is a type which is carved into grotesque and amusing little figures, having glass eyes and perhaps a silver mouth.

(Above) *Charles II bead stumpwork casket, the lid showing the King and Queen Catherine standing in an arbour, below a fruiting vine; on the sides and front reliefs of Flora and Juno; and on the back a stumpwork castle with free-standing castellation and a hinged door, a leopard and stag on either side. 11 ins. long.* (Sotheby & Co.)

(Below) *Charles I beadwork casket, the top with a lady and gentleman in court costume, the front with a lion and a unicorn and a dog chasing a hare; the back with a stag and griffin; the sides with birds, a squirrel, and insects. 15 ins. wide.* (Sotheby & Co.)

(Above) *South Indian carved sandalwood. Nineteenth century.* (Victoria & Albert Museum.)
(Below) *Wooden casket covered with silver foil showing cartouche work and gadrooning. German seventeenth century. 3½ ins. high.* (Victoria & Albert Museum.)

They are sometimes taken to be made of burr wood; but this is something quite different. Burr or burl wood is an excrescence on a tree, usually where a branch has been lost.

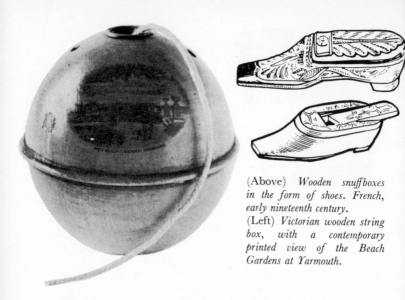

(Above) *Wooden snuffboxes in the form of shoes. French, early nineteenth century.*
(Left) *Victorian wooden string box, with a contemporary printed view of the Beach Gardens at Yarmouth.*

Because the fibres of wood grow in all directions they are peculiarly free from warping and distortion, and so make good material for carving and for mounting with silver. Walnut, elm, ash, and maple are all subject to burrs, but apparently the makers like birch and maple best. Designs are impressed by steam on the lids and bottoms—hunting scenes, allegorical subjects, double heads, historical scenes, all appear frequently on the covers, but the bases usually have geometrical designs.

Boxes of pressed horn are often found; they were especially popular in France for commemorating events. Among the many carved in wood are those shaped as shoes, sometimes said to be the passing-out pieces by cobbler apprentices; some of these have mother-of-pearl hearts on them—with different initials on each shoe. There are the little boxes with Welsh geometric carving, pottery money boxes from Staffordshire, Wedgwood jasper ware boxes for the toilet table . . . but the list is endless, and would need another book to complete.